Contents

DID YOU KNOW? Discover amazing facts about electricity.

THE SCIENCE OF ELECTRICITY

Find out more about the science of electricity.

ELECTRICITY FIRSTS

Learn more about electricity inventions and discoveries.

1ST

Some words are shown in bold, **like this**. You can find out what they mean by looking in the glossary.

Where does electricity come from?

The electricity that powers an electric car comes from many different places. The story of one of these journeys begins with a shower of rain falling from a cloud.

Every activity you can think of needs **energy**. Every time you stand up, or the wind blows, or the Sun warms your skin, or a ball rolls down a hill, energy is being used. Even when you are asleep, you are using energy. Energy is the ability to do things. Nothing can happen without it. There are many different forms of energy. Electricity, heat and light are just three of them. Every moving object has another type of energy called **kinetic energy**.

▲ Some of the energy that will be used by an electric car begins its journey in a raincloud in the sky.

From
Falling Water
to
Electric Car

An Energy Journey Through the World of Electricity

Ian Graham

raintree

a Capstone company — publishers for children

Raintree is an imprint of Capstone Global Library Limited, a company incorporated in England and Wales having its registered office at 7 Pilgrim Street, London, EC4V 6LB – Registered company number: 6695582

www.raintreepublishers.co.uk
myorders@raintreepublishers.co.uk

Edited by Linda Staniford and Anthony Wacholtz
Designed by Steve Mead
Original illustrations © Capstone Global Library 2015
Illustrated by HL Studios
Picture research by Eric Gohl
Production by Helen McCreath
Originated by Capstone Global Library Ltd
Printed and bound in China by CTPS

ISBN 978 1 406 28962 6
18 17 16 15 14
10 9 8 7 6 5 4 3 2 1

British Library Cataloguing in Publication Data
A full catalogue record for this book is available from the British Library.

Acknowledgements
We would like to thank the following for permission to reproduce photographs: Alamy: Novarc Images, cover (bottom), Phil Degginger, 39 (bottom), Simon Clay, 28; Capstone: 19; Corbis: Imaginechina, 8, Robert Llewellyn, 23; Dreamstime: Jorg Hackemann, 34; Getty Images: Gamma-Keystone, 35; Newscom: Ingram Publishing, 25, Stock Connection Worldwide/Andre Jenny, 11, ZUMA Press/David Cooper, 37; Science Source: Dr. John Brackenbury, 7, Martyn F. Chillmaid, 21; Shutterstock: Chatchai Somwat, 41, Chimponzee, 10, coloursinmylife, 16, czdast, 33, djgis, 42, Dong Liu, 36, Esteban De Armas, 43, Gio.tto, 27, Huguette Roe, 40, imagedb.com, 32, Ivan Montero Martinez, 20, kavram, 4, Lena Pan, 26, NCG, 17, photoiconix, cover (top), Photo Works, 9, Ralf Broskvar, 12, Roblan, 6, saiko3p, 5, stocker1970, 18, Sylvie Bouchard, 22, Yogibehr, 29, Zhu Difeng, 24.

We would like to thank Patrick O'Mahony for his help in the preparation of this book.

Every effort has been made to contact copyright holders of material reproduced in this book. Any omissions will be rectified in subsequent printings if notice is given to the publisher.

Changing energy

Energy cannot be created or destroyed. It can only be changed from one form to another. Energy will change from one form to another many times during its journey from a rain shower to an electric car.

An everyday raincloud measuring 1 kilometre (3,300 feet) across can weigh as much as 1 million tonnes! A cloud forms when warm air rises and cools down in the colder conditions high above the ground. When moisture in the rising air cools down, it changes into tiny water droplets or ice crystals. These scatter sunlight in all directions and this is why clouds look white or grey.

▲ Shop signs glow brightly because they change electrical energy into light.

Does rain have energy?

*Raindrops have a type of energy called **potential energy**. Potential energy is stored energy. It is energy that is waiting to do something. As raindrops fall to the ground, pulled down by **gravity**, their potential energy changes into kinetic energy. This is the type of energy that all moving things have.*

The raindrops have some heat energy, too. As they fall, they move from very cold air high in the sky into warmer air close to the ground. On the way, they take in some heat energy from the warmer air.

▼ Raindrops carry useful amounts of energy that can be converted into other forms of energy.

Flowing downhill

Raindrops that fall on the ground might be lapped up from a puddle by a passing dog, or they might fall on someone's head. The droplets that will power an electric car fall into a river. Rivers flow downhill. As the raindrops flow downhill in the river, more of their potential energy changes into kinetic energy.

Scientists in France have made electricity from the energy in falling rain. The raindrops fall on a special material that produces a tiny burst of electricity every time a raindrop hits it. One raindrop produces very little electricity, but thousands of raindrops falling every second could light a small bulb.

▲ One raindrop has enough energy to knock down a large insect. A shower of rain has billions of times the energy of one raindrop, if only we could find a way to collect the energy and use it.

Rivers to reservoirs

A river might flow all the way to the sea, or it might flow into a giant lake called a reservoir. A reservoir is a lake that is used for storing water needed by people. The water you use for drinking, washing and cooking probably comes from a reservoir.

Some reservoirs are lakes created by nature. Nature does not always make reservoirs where they are needed, so some reservoirs have to be built. A wall is built across a river valley to hold the river back. The wall is called a dam. Water piles up behind the dam and fills the valley.

▲ Water flowing through a dam has an enormous amount of kinetic energy that can be converted into electricity.

The biggest reservoir in the United States is Lake Mead. Part of it is in the state of Arizona and the rest is in Nevada. It contains enough water to flood land more than twice the size of the Republic of Ireland, to a depth of 30 centimetres (12 inches).

▲ The Hoover Dam in the United States holds back the Colorado River. The water that piles up behind the dam forms a reservoir called Lake Mead.

Making electricity

Some reservoirs send water to power stations for making electricity. Electricity made from water is called **hydroelectricity**. At a hydroelectric power station, water from the reservoir flows into a huge pipe called a penstock that goes through the dam. Some of the energy in this flowing water will be changed into electrical energy.

How is electricity made from water?

*Somehow, the kinetic energy in the water flowing through the dam has to be changed into electrical energy. The water will have to give up its energy to a machine. A circular motion is the best for powering machines, but the water is travelling in a straight line. The answer is a **turbine**.*

◄ People have used waterwheels to take energy from moving water for more than 2,000 years.

ELECTRICITY FIRSTS 1ST

The world's first hydroelectric power station opened in 1882 on the Fox River in Appleton, Wisconsin, USA. It produced just enough electricity to light the power station, the home of the man who built it, and a nearby building. Today, nearly a fifth of all the electricity generated all over the world is hydroelectricity.

What does a turbine do?

A turbine looks like a drum with blades or paddles sticking out all around it. It works like a very fast waterwheel. When moving water hits its blades, the water gives up some of its kinetic energy to the blades and they start moving. The turbine spins.

The water's job is now finished. It flows out into the valley on the other side of the dam and continues its journey to the sea.

blades

➤ Turbines work like ancient waterwheels, but turbines are designed to work with much faster-flowing water.

The Itaipu hydroelectric power station is one of the biggest in the world. It stands on the Paraná River, on the border between Brazil and Paraguay in South America. A line of 20 penstocks (huge pipes) guide water to its turbines. About 690,000 litres (182,000 US gallons) of water rush through each penstock every second. That is enough to fill more than 30,000 baths every second!

Generating electricity

The spinning turbine powers a machine called a **generator**. The generator's job is to change the kinetic energy of the turbine into electrical energy.

◄ The turbine hall of a hydroelectric power station has a row of generators driven by spinning turbines below them.

How does a generator work?

A generator makes electricity by using magnetism. When a wire moves near a magnet, magnetic forces make an **electric current** flow along the wire. A generator has a magnet in the middle that can spin. The magnet has coils of wire wrapped around it. When a turbine spins the magnet inside the wire coils, magnetic forces make an electric current flow through the wire.

ELECTRICITY FIRSTS

The electricity generator was invented in 1831 by a British scientist, Michael Faraday. He built a small working model. But it was a Frenchman, Hippolyte Pixii, who in 1832 built the first generator that could produce enough electricity to do useful work.

1ST

An electric current flows out of a power station's generators. The energy's journey has taken one more step. It has changed from potential energy into kinetic energy, and now it has changed into electrical energy.

The link between electricity and magnetism was discovered by accident! A Danish scientist called Hans Christian Oersted was showing his students an experiment in 1820. Every time he switched an electric current on or off, he noticed that a magnetic compass needle nearby twitched. It showed that electricity and magnetism affect each other. This simple discovery made it possible to invent **electric motors**, generators and other electrical machines.

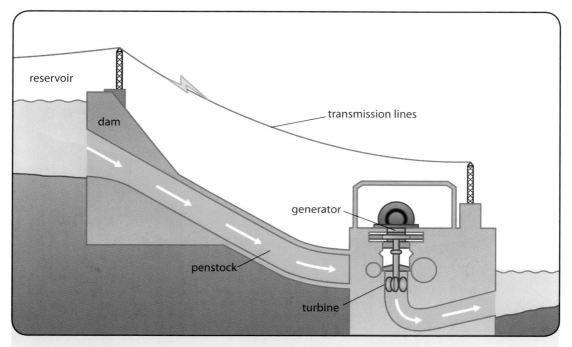

▲ A hydroelectric power station uses the energy in moving water to make electricity.

MAKE A WATER TURBINE

You can make your own water turbine from a cotton reel and some cardboard, and then see how it takes energy from flowing water.

You will need:
- **cotton reel**
- **round pencil or knitting needle**
- **card**
- **glue**
- **scissors.**

Making it work

1 Cut out four pieces of card, each about 3.5 centimetres (1.5 inches) long by 2.5 centimetres (1 inch) wide.

2 Fold a piece of card in two and glue one half of it to the cotton reel. Repeat this for the other three cards, to form a turbine with four blades.

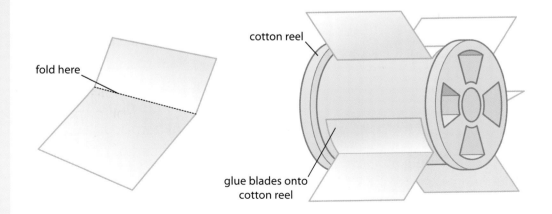

fold here

cotton reel

glue blades onto cotton reel

3 When the glue is dry, push a pencil or knitting needle through the middle of the cotton reel. Make sure the cotton reel can spin freely and easily.

4 Hold the cotton reel turbine under a running tap and watch it spin.

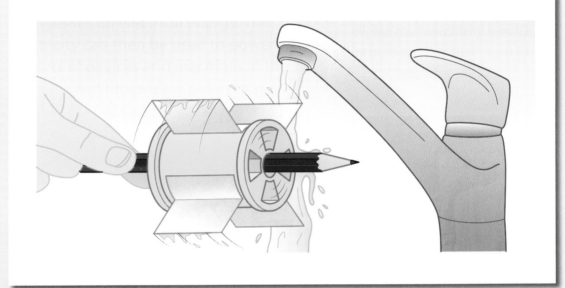

What happened?

The water falling from the tap has kinetic energy. When it hits the turbine blades, it gives up some of its kinetic energy to them. It is this energy that makes the turbine spin.

Now try making another turbine with more blades, and perhaps another one with curved blades instead of straight blades. Which turbine spins fastest? Colouring one of the blades with a waterproof pen or crayon makes it easier to see which turbine is spinning faster.

Do you think the size of the blades makes any difference? Will bigger blades catch more water, take more energy from it and spin the turbine faster? Try it and see.

Other power stations

Most power stations do not work like hydroelectric power stations. The energy they change into electrical energy comes from burning coal or gas instead of from flowing water. The burning **fuel** heats water to make steam. Then the steam spins a turbine, which powers a generator.

Nuclear power stations use the heat from a fuel called uranium, but they do not have to burn the uranium. Uranium is made of big **atoms** that split apart easily. When they split apart they give out a tiny burst of heat energy. They also send out particles that split more uranium atoms, making more heat. The heat is used to make steam that drives a turbine and generator.

▲ Power stations that use steam to make electricity work like giant kettles.

Renewable energy

Wind, waves, sunlight and other natural processes contain energy that can be changed into electrical energy. These are often called renewables, because they are constantly renewed by nature.

Now we have electrical energy, but it is not where it is needed. The next step is to move the energy to the places where people can use it.

DID YOU KNOW?

The world's biggest wind turbines are giants. Some of them stand 198 metres (650 feet) high and their blades are 127 metres (417 feet) across. Each of these wind turbines can supply enough electricity for 5,000 homes. The turbine and the massive concrete block it stands on weigh 6,000 tonnes (6,600 tons).

spinning blades

generator

tower

▲ The spinning blades of a wind turbine power a generator in the cabin at the top of the tower.

How is electricity moved around?

The electrical energy from a power station is moved to where it is needed by sending it along cables called **transmission lines.** *As the electric current flows along a transmission line, some of its energy changes into heat, which escapes into the surrounding air. Less energy is lost in this way if the electricity is at a very high* **voltage.** *But if the voltage is too high, the electricity can flow out into the air. So, electricity is sent along transmission lines at more than 100,000* **volts** *but less than 2 million volts.*

◄ The cables that move electrical energy from place to place are strung between tall metal towers called pylons. These keep the cables at a safe distance above the ground.

Boosting voltage

The electricity is boosted to a high voltage by a **transformer**. An electric current flowing through a coil of wire in the transformer creates magnetism around the coil. This makes an electric current flow through a second coil of wire in the transformer. The voltage of the electricity in the second coil can be made higher or lower than in the first coil.

▲ The little plastic plug-in box that charges a mobile phone has a transformer inside it. It changes the supply voltage to the lower voltage that charges the **battery**.

THE SCIENCE OF ⚡ ELECTRICITY

In 1831, English scientist Michael Faraday discovered that a coil of wire becomes magnetic when an electric current flows through it. The coil behaves like a magnet. He also found that this electric magnet, or **electromagnet**, could make an electric current flow in a nearby coil of wire. He had discovered electromagnetic induction, the principle behind the operation of the transformer.

Volts and amps

Electricity is described using words like volts and **amps**, but what do they mean? The number of volts shows the size of the electric force pushing an electric current around a circuit. The current, measured in amps, shows how much electric charge is flowing every second.

▲ This 1.5-volt battery is a popular choice for powering small toys, torches and clocks.

DID YOU KNOW?

Volts are named after Italian scientist Alessandro Volta, the inventor of the battery. Amps are named after André-Marie Ampère, a French scientist who studied electricity and magnetism. The **watt** is named after James Watt, a Scottish engineer who designed steam engines.

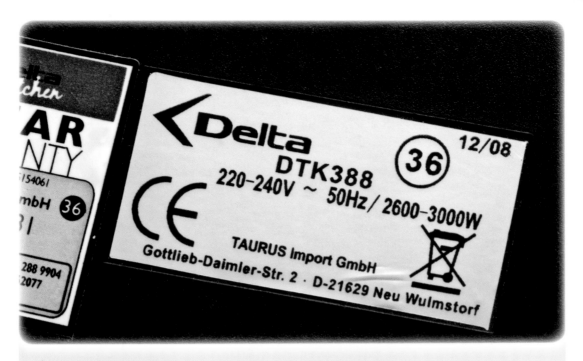

▲ Electrical devices such as kettles and ovens are marked with the number of volts they need and their power in watts.

Imagine water flowing through a hose instead of an electric current flowing around a circuit. Opening the tap to start the water flowing is like switching on the power to start the electric current flowing. The pushing force of the water from the tap is like the electric force, or voltage, of a battery. The amount of water flowing through the hose every second is like the electric current flowing in a circuit.

THE SCIENCE OF ELECTRICITY

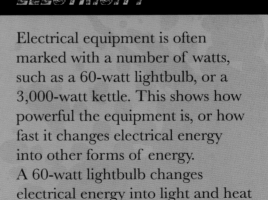

Electrical equipment is often marked with a number of watts, such as a 60-watt lightbulb, or a 3,000-watt kettle. This shows how powerful the equipment is, or how fast it changes electrical energy into other forms of energy. A 60-watt lightbulb changes electrical energy into light and heat twice as fast as a 30-watt bulb, so the 60-watt bulb is brighter.

Lowering the volts

The high-voltage electricity sent along a transmission line cannot be used at home. The voltage is far too high. This high-voltage electricity must be lowered from hundreds of thousands of volts to a safer level for the home. In the United States and Canada, this is about 120 volts. In Britain, Europe and Australia, it is about 230 volts. The voltage is not lowered all at once. It is brought down in steps by a series of transformers called substations. Finally, the electricity is at the correct voltage to be supplied to homes.

High and low

In some places, the power cables that carry electricity on the last part of its journey to people's homes are above the ground. They are strung between tall poles to keep them safely out of reach. In towns and cities, these power cables are usually buried underground.

◄ These drums are a common sight in parts of the United States, where they lower the electricity supply to the voltage used in homes.

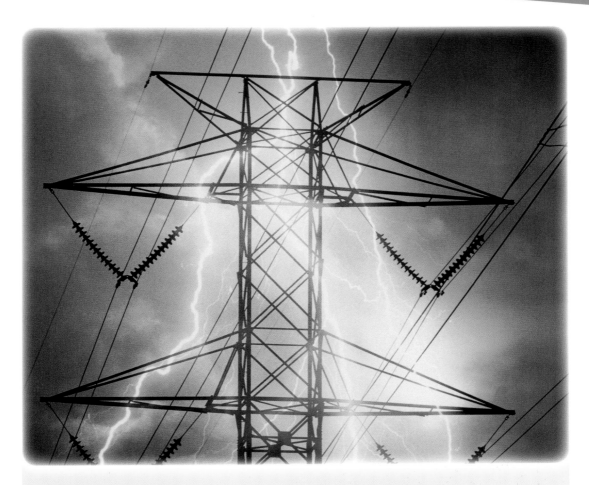

▲ Power cables and the tall metal towers they hang from are sometimes hit by lightning. Safety devices stop the lightning from travelling along the lines to people's homes.

There are two types of electric current. They are called DC and AC. The electric current from a battery always flows in the same direction. This is Direct Current, or DC. The electricity from a wall socket is different. Its current changes direction, forwards and backwards, 50 or 60 times every second. This is Alternating Current, or AC.

Making cars

Some of the electrical energy from power stations is sent to car factories, where it is used to build cars.

Sheets of steel are cut and bent into the shape of panels for making a car's body. The parts of the body are joined together by welding. The steel panels are held together and then a big electric current is passed through them. The electrical energy changes into so much heat that the two pieces of metal melt together and become one.

▲ Imagine the huge amount of energy needed to melt metal to make iron and steel for building cars.

Did You Know?

Hyundai's factory in Ulsan, South Korea, is the world's biggest car factory. It makes 6,000 cars a day, or about 1.5 million cars a year. It has its own dock where ships arrive to take the cars away for sale all over the world.

The car bodies move along an electrically powered track called an assembly line. As they move along, workers add more and more parts to them. By the time each car reaches the end of the line, it is finished and a worker drives it away for tests.

A lot of energy goes into building a car. Some of it is stored in the car's battery. So how does the battery use it?

▲ Sparks fly when the robots in a car factory convert electrical energy into heat for welding pieces of metal together.

How do cars make electricity?

Before a car can go anywhere, the engine has to be started. The energy needed to start the engine is stored in the car's battery. The battery powers a small electric motor that starts the engine. It also powers the lights, radio and other equipment when the engine is not running.

When the engine starts, it powers a small generator, also called an **alternator**. The alternator takes over the job of running the car's electrical equipment. It also produces enough energy to charge the battery so that it is ready to start the engine next time.

▼ Car batteries make electricity by using metal plates in acid, in the same way as Volta's battery (see page 27).

battery

How do batteries work?

A battery has two **electrical terminals**, called the **anode** and the **cathode**. The cathode has lots of extra particles called **electrons**. Each electron has a negative electric charge, so the cathode is negative. The anode is short of electrons, so the anode is positive. The electrons would like to get from the cathode to the anode. The car's lights, radio and other electrical equipment are connected to these terminals. When a piece of equipment is switched on, electrons travel from the cathode to the anode by flowing through the equipment and making it work.

➤ The battery invented by Alessandro Volta was the first practical device that could supply a steady electric current.

ELECTRICITY FIRSTS

1ST

The battery was invented by Italian scientist Alessandro Volta in 1800. His battery was a pile of copper and zinc plates. Pads between the metal plates were soaked in salty water or acid. Chemical reactions between the metal and salty water or acid made the pile work as a battery.

Electric pathways

For a car's electrical equipment to work as it should, the electric current that brings it to life has to be guided along the correct path. The path is called an electric circuit.

Conductors and insulators

The materials that an electric circuit is made of are carefully chosen to make sure that the electric current follows the correct path. Some materials let an electric current flow through them, but others do not. Materials that electric currents flow through are called **conductors**. Materials that electric currents cannot flow through are called **insulators**.

▲ The wires used in a car's electrical circuits are covered with different coloured plastic insulators to make it easier to work out which wire is which.

▲ Plugs and sockets used for high-quality sound and video equipment often have gold-plated electrical contacts, because gold is a very good conductor of electricity.

The wires that an electric current flow along are covered with plastic. The current flows through the metal in the middle of the wires, but not through the plastic covering. The current goes only where it is meant to go. Without the plastic covering on the wires, the current would leak out of the circuit into any metal parts of the car that the wires touched.

DID YOU KNOW?

Gold and silver are very good electrical conductors, but they are far too expensive for making everyday electrical wiring, circuits and equipment. Instead, a cheaper metal called copper is used. Copper is ideal for making electrical wiring because it is strong, it bends easily without breaking and it does not rust like iron and steel.

MAKE A CONDUCTOR-INSULATOR TESTER

Do you know which materials are conductors and which are insulators? You can make a tester to find out.

You will need:
- **kitchen foil**
- **torch bulb**
- **clothes peg**
- **1.5-volt D-cell battery**
- **sticky tape.**

Making it work

1 Take a piece of kitchen foil 15 centimetres (6 inches) long. Fold it in half again and again until it is a strip no more than about 12 millimetres (half an inch) wide.

2 Wrap one end of the foil strip around the metal base of the torch bulb. Use the clothes peg to hold it in place.

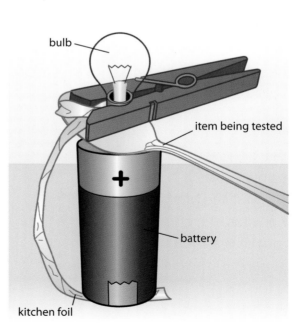

bulb

item being tested

battery

kitchen foil

3 Fasten the other end of the foil strip to the flat base of the battery with sticky tape.

Using your tester

Take an item you want to test, such as a spoon. Place it between the bulb and battery. Make sure the bulb is pressed tightly onto the item, and the item is pressed tightly onto the button-shaped contact on top of the battery. If the bulb lights, the item is a conductor. If it does not light, the item is an insulator. You could test items such as a pencil, a key, a coin, a piece of card and a plastic ruler.

What happened?

The battery, foil and bulb form an electric circuit. Electric current flows from the battery, through the foil and bulb, and back to the battery. As the current flows through the bulb, some electrical energy is converted into light and heat, making the bulb light up. If the item being tested is a conductor, an electric current flows through it and lights the bulb. If the item is an insulator, the electric current will not flow through it and the bulb does not light up.

Finding faults

If an electric circuit is faulty, it might be dangerous to use. To solve this problem, electric circuits are fitted with safety devices called **fuses**. The simplest fuse is a thin piece of wire. If too much current flows through a circuit, some of its electrical energy changes into heat in the fuse. The thin fuse wire heats up so much that it melts and switches the current off.

Breaking circuits

Electric circuits in homes are often fitted with **circuit breakers** instead of fuses. A circuit breaker is a special type of switch. If too much electric current flows through it, the extra, unwanted electrical energy changes into heat or magnetic energy, which throws the switch and cuts off the current. When the fault is fixed, the circuit breaker is switched on again.

➤ The thin wire inside a fuse melts if too much electric current flows through it.

Cars use electrical energy in all sorts of different ways, and their circuits are protected by fuses, too.

THE SCIENCE OF ELECTRICITY

If a conductor is very thin, like a fuse wire, electrons cannot travel through it easily. It is like trying to push a lot of water through a very thin pipe. In the fuse wire, the electrons are slowed down and they lose kinetic energy. The energy has to go somewhere, so it changes to heat in the fuse wire, which melts.

▲ Fuses are often made in different colours, like these car fuses. The colour shows how much current a fuse will let through before it melts and switches the circuit off.

How do cars use electricity?

A car changes electrical energy into all sorts of different forms of energy. The car's lights change it into light. The horn changes it into sound. The heater changes it into heat. The radio changes it into sound. The windscreen wiper motor changes it into the movement of wipers across the windscreen to sweep rain away. Cars with air conditioning use electrical energy to pump heat out of the car and keep it cool inside. The engine has to be kept cool, too. An electric pump pushes water around the engine. If the water does not cool the engine enough, an electric fan switches on to blow air around the engine.

▼ Bright electric headlights make it possible to drive cars safely on dark roads by changing electrical energy into light.

Making sparks

Cars with petrol, or gasoline, engines need electric sparks to burn fuel inside the engine. The car's **ignition** system produces the sparks. At top speed, it has to produce hundreds of sparks every second. Each spark burns a small amount of fuel. The burning fuel heats air inside the engine. The air heats up and expands. The pushing force of the hot air makes the engine run and turns the car's wheels.

Cars had starting handles until the 1950s! If a car's battery was flat (had used all of its stored energy) or the starter motor didn't work, the engine could be started by turning the handle. Chemical energy in the driver's muscles took the place of electrical energy from the battery.

▲ In the early days of motoring, cars had starting handles. Instead of power coming from the battery to start the engine, the driver would turn the handle. Modern cars have starter motors which are powered by the battery.

Electric cars

Some of the energy that started its journey in a shower of rain is used to make all-electric cars. These cars have no engine. Instead, a big battery powers an electric motor that turns the car's wheels.

▲ When an electric car's battery uses up all the energy stored inside it, it has to be refilled with energy, or recharged. This is done by plugging it into an electricity supply.

DID YOU KNOW?

A car's brakes work by changing the car's kinetic energy into heat. Air flowing around the brakes carries the heat away, so it ends up warming the air. What a waste! Electric cars have brakes that save this energy. When the car brakes, its kinetic energy is changed into electricity, which charges the car's battery. Then this energy can be used again by the car.

Hybrid cars

Another type of electric car has an engine as well as a big battery. This is called a **hybrid electric car**. The battery powers the car for short trips. For longer journeys and higher speeds, or when the battery is running out of energy, the driver can switch to the engine. The engine also powers a generator that recharges the battery. So, a hybrid car does not have to stop to recharge its battery.

This energy journey does not end here. The energy continues on its way, being changed into other forms of energy and used again and again.

▲ This looks like an ordinary car, but it is actually a hybrid electric car. It can be powered by a battery or by an engine.

MAKE AN ELECTROMAGNET

Would you like to make your own electromagnet? This is a magnet that uses electricity to create magnetism. You can turn it on and off.

You will need:
- **a 1.5-volt D-cell battery (WARNING: do not use a rechargeable battery for this activity)**
- **iron or steel nail about 15 centimetres (6 inches) long**
- **1 metre (3 feet) of plastic-covered wire**
- **steel paperclips**
- **sticky tape.**

Making it work

1 Wind the wire tightly around the whole length of the nail about 10 times. Use sticky tape to hold the wire in place on the nail.

2 Hold one end of the wire on one battery terminal, and the other end of the wire on the other terminal. If the battery or wire gets hot, disconnect them.

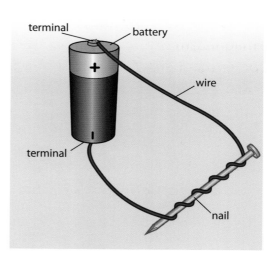

terminal · battery · wire · terminal · nail

3 Dip one end of the nail into a pile of paperclips. How many paperclips did it pick up?

4 Wrap another 10 turns of wire around the whole length of the nail. How many paperclips can you pick up now?

At the end of the experiment, disconnect the wire from the battery.

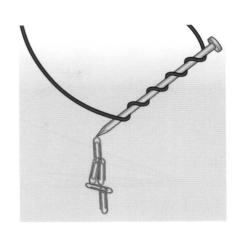

What happened?

An electromagnet changes electrical energy to magnetic energy. This is the same process that goes on inside a motor, generator and transformer. When an electric current flows through a wire, some of the electrical energy is changed into magnetism. When the wire is wound around a nail, the nail makes the magnetism stronger. The nail itself becomes magnetised. This type of magnet, called an electromagnet, can be switched on and off.

▲ Can your electromagnet pick up as many paperclips as this?

DID YOU KNOW?

Electromagnets are used in motors and generators. They also operate the electric door-locks in cars. In scrapyards, a powerful electromagnet hanging from a crane is often used to lift heavy scrap metal and move it around. Electromagnets also provide the power to lift trains called **maglevs** above their special track and also move them along the track.

Recycling energy

At the end of a car's working life, some of the energy that went into building it and running it can be saved and used again. More than half of a car is made of steel. This can be recycled (used again).

When a car is too old, worn out or broken to be used any more, it is taken to a scrapyard. All the useful parts are taken off it. Some of these can be used again in other cars. Then the steel body is crushed to make it smaller. Lots of crushed car bodies are loaded onto a truck and taken to a place where steel is made. The old steel is mixed with new steel in a **furnace**. The furnace is so hot that all the steel melts and runs together. Some of this steel is used to make new cars. Recycling old steel again like this saves energy that would have been needed to make new steel.

▲ Recycling one car saves more than 1,134 kilograms (2,500 pounds) of iron ore, 635 kilograms (1,400 pounds) of coal and 54 kilograms (120 pounds) of limestone.

▲ Some of the energy that started its journey in a shower of rain ends up helping to build another new car.

DID YOU KNOW?

More than 12 million old cars are recycled in the United States every year. This produces up to 13.6 million tonnes (15 million tons) of scrap steel that can be used again. About a quarter of the steel in every new car has been used at least once before.

What have we learned about electricity?

After following energy on its journey from a shower of rain to an electric car, we have learned that:

- *electricity is one of many different forms of energy*
- *it is a very useful form of energy because it can be moved from place to place easily, stored in batteries and changed into all sorts of other forms of energy including heat, light, sound and movement.*

➤ Most of the energy we use on Earth comes from the Sun.

Never-ending energy

Energy has been changing from one form to another and moving from place to place since the Universe began more than 13 billion years ago. The energy used by a car today might have arrived on Earth from the Sun as **solar energy** billions of years ago.

Hundreds of millions of years ago, it might have become the electrical energy in a flash of lightning. A million years ago, it might have become the kinetic energy of ocean waves crashing onto the shore. Today, it could be the electrical energy that starts a car. In future, it might become waves of radio energy carrying a message to an astronaut standing on Mars.

DID YOU KNOW?

Every time energy is used, a little of it changes into one or more unwanted forms. For example, a lightbulb's job is to convert electrical energy into light, but some of it changes into heat. Unwanted energy changes like this are called losses. Designers of devices and machines try to keep energy losses as small as possible.

▲ The electrical energy you are using today might be used by an astronaut on Mars one day.

Glossary

alternator electricity generator that produces alternating current, which is then changed to direct current to recharge a car's battery

amp unit of electric current

anode positive electrical terminal

atom basic building block of matter

battery device that supplies electrical energy, which it stores as chemical energy

cathode negative electrical terminal

circuit breaker safety device that switches off an electric circuit if the circuit suffers a dangerous fault

conductor material that allows heat or electricity to pass through it easily

electric current flow of electric charges

electric motor machine that changes electrical energy into kinetic energy

electrical terminal connector for linking electrical conductors together

electromagnet type of magnet created by an electric current flowing through a coil of wire

electron particle of matter with a negative electric charge

energy ability to do work, measured in joules

fuel material such as coal or uranium containing energy that can be converted into heat energy

furnace device or container that is heated to a very high temperature

fuse safety device that stops a dangerously high electric current flowing in a faulty electric circuit

generator machine for producing electricity

gravity force that pulls everything down to the ground

hybrid electric car car that can be powered by an electric motor or an engine

hydroelectricity electricity produced from the energy in moving water

ignition setting something on fire, such as the fuel inside an engine

insulator material that does not let heat or electricity flow through it easily or quickly

kinetic energy movement energy

maglev short for magnetic levitation, a kind of train that runs on electromagnetic suspension

potential energy energy stored in an object

solar energy energy given out by the Sun, mainly light and heat

transformer device that changes the voltage of electricity

transmission line long cable carrying high-voltage electricity

turbine drum or disc with blades sticking out all around it, like a propeller with lots of blades, that spins like a waterwheel to create kinetic energy

volt unit of electrical force

voltage difference in energy that electrical charges have between two points

watt unit of power

Find out more

Books

Charging About: The Story of Electricity (Science Works), Jacqui Bailey
  (A&C Black, 2013)
Electricity (Eyewitness), Steve Parker (Dorling Kindersley, 2013)
Electricity (How Does My Home Work?), Chris Oxlade (Raintree, 2013)
Electricity (Project Science), Sally Hewitt (Franklin Watts, 2012)
Electricity (Super Science), Rob Colson (Franklin Watts, 2013)
Solar Power (Tales of Invention), Chris Oxlade (Raintree, 2012)
Using Electricity (It's Electric!), Chris Oxlade (Raintree, 2013)

Websites

http://auto.howstuffworks.com/fuel-efficiency/vehicles/electric-car-battery.htm
Use this website to find out more about how car batteries work.

http://www.powerup.ukpowernetworks.co.uk/under-11.aspx/
On this website you can read about electricity, where it comes from, and
how it is used, from the UK Power Networks.

http://www.explainthatstuff.com/electricity.html
Here you can learn more about all sorts of electricity.

http://kidshealth.org/kid/talk/qa/electric_shock.html
If you want to know more about static electricity, have a look at this website.

Places to visit

Green Britain Centre

Swaffham, Norfolk, PE37 7HT

At this centre you can climb to the top of the only wind turbine in the world that is open to the public. You can also see how solar energy is used to make electricity.

www.greenbritaincentre.co.uk

Science Museum

Exhibition Road, South Kensington, London, SW7 2DD

The Science Museum is a very good place to visit to find out about any science or technology topic, including electricity. Look on the website for details of special events, shows and exhibitions.

http://www.sciencemuseum.org.uk

Further research

There is a lot more to learn about electricity. Here are some ideas for topics to research.

- Did you know that your body works because of electricity? You can see, hear, smell and feel because of electric currents flowing from all parts of your body to your brain. And you can move because of electric currents flowing back from your brain to your muscles. Find out how your body uses electricity.

- You could find out more about other examples of electricity in nature, such as lightning. How many flashes of lightning are there all over the world every day? Where is lightning most common and what causes it?

- Did you know that light and radio waves are partly electrical and partly magnetic? They are called electromagnetic waves. You can see the Sun, Moon and distant stars because of these energy waves. Find out more about electromagnetic waves.

Index